Lotus Path: Practicing the Lotus Sutra

Volume 3
by
Ryusho Jeffus

Cover photo copyright Ryusho Jeffus 2019 - Black Water Swamp, South Carolina USA

Lotus Path: Practicing the Lotus Sutra
Volume 3

By Ryusho Jeffus

Copyright 2019

Myosho-ji, Wonderful Voice Buddhist Temple
611 Vine3 St.
Syracuse, NY 13203 USA

License Notes

All rights reserved under International and Pan-American Copyright Conventions. This book, or parts thereof, may not be reproduced in any form without written permission except by a reviewer who may quote brief passages in a review. All photographs, including cover are by Ryusho Jeffus and may not be reproduced without written permission.

ISBN: 9781691717224
Imprint: Independently published

Quotations from the Lotus Sutra:
The Lotus Sutra
The Sutra of the Lotus Flower of the Wonderful Dharma
Translated from Kumarajiva's version of
The Saddharmapundarika-Sutra
Third Edition
by Senchu Murano
Copyright 2012 Nichiren Shu

More Books by Rysuho Jeffus:

Lecture on the Lotus Sutra

Lotus Sutra Practice Guide

Important Matters

Daily Lotus

Incarcerated Lotus

The Magic City

The Physician's Good Medicine

Lotus Path Vol 1 & 2

Contemplating Disease

King Wonderful Adornment

Lire du Sutra du Lotus

Cité Magique

Le Bon Remède du Médecin Habile

Roi Ornement-Merveilleux

Cuestiones Importantes: Sutra del Loto, Fé y Práctica

Disertaciones sobre el Sutra del Loto

Dear Reader:

Thank you for purchasing this book of essays, which I hope will help you deepen your faith in and practice of Nichiren Buddhism. I also hope this book may be a catalyst in helping you make changes in your life so you can become happy in the Dharma of the Lotus Sutra and enlightened.

The practice of Buddhism is about changing our lives deep at the core. Buddhism calls on us to examine the causes of our suffering in brutal honesty. After making this self-assessment we then take the next step and make the necessary changes so we can free ourselves from the cycle of suffering in ignorance.

The essays in the book are short; usually only several hundred words. It is possible to read them quite quickly, although that runs counter to our contemplative inner work.

You will get the most value out of this book if you take your time and use the essays and the follow-up comments as tools. Use the book sparingly, sampling each essay as if it were a most delicious candy. This book will be of the most value to you if you actually try to use it as a tool for making changes in your life.

Please take your time and enjoy these essays. I hope they encourage you to deepen your faith and practice of the Lotus Sutra.

With Gassho
Ryusho Jeffus - Kansho Shonin

Contents

Appreciation; Spiritual Progress

Appreciation; Spiritual Progress – September 9, 2012
Meditation

Lack of appreciation starves us of joy and closes us off
from learning. If we fail to take notice of the things that
make our life possible then we may all too easily think
we are the center of the universe and our needs are more
important than those of others.

The fact that we are able to breathe, are able to be
conscious, and that we have life is truly a remarkable
thing. There are countless small things without which
our lives would be dramatically different if even existing
at all. If we take the time to open up our lives to all the
subtle things up which we depend we are able to experience
appreciation, which potentially allows us to experience joy.

An open and appreciative life realizes that every experience
is an opportunity to learn, to grow, and to change.

> *"He later planted the roots of good, and became
> able to see many hundreds of thousands of billions
> of Buddhas. He made offerings to them, respected
> them, honored them, and praised them." (Lotus
> Sutra, Chapter I)*

In a previous life Maitreya was named Fame-Seeking because he was attached to gain and did not take seriously the study of the Sutras. Even when he did study he forgot much of what he learned, he was focused on himself.

When we become so attached to our own self, ignoring the contributions of countless others to our very existence, when we forget to express gratitude for the things we have been given, we are forgetting the teachings of the Dharma given by the Buddha. We become like Fame-Seeking.

However, just as the sutra says, we can plant the roots of good, we can open ourselves up to appreciate the many ways the universe supports our life. When we look around us with the mind of appreciation then we to will be able to see countless Buddhas who surround us and who support us.

Are You Ready

Are You Ready – January 1, 2012

Happy New Year! As I look forward to what might be in store for this new year, I realize I have absolutely no idea. Isn't that pretty neat?

All of our lives we have to "be ready." As children we have to be ready for dinner, washing hands, or just being on time. We had to be ready for school, get our homework done, or catch the bus. Then we grow older and even as adults we have to be ready for work, tie on straight, no wrinkles in our slacks, hair neat. We spend a large portion of our lives getting ready for things. Many of the things we prepare for we know exactly what to expect.

It is harder to prepare for what we don't know will happen. So what's the best way to prepare for the unknown?

In the Lotus Sutra the elders of the Sangha, who felt they were too old and had settled for the attainment of Nirvana only said to the Buddha:

> "...you did a rare thing.
> You prepared us with expedients, And then taught us
> the great wisdom." (Lotus Sutra, Chapter IV)

Sometimes, when we don't know what the future will hold for us we default to doing things just the way we have in the past. In Buddhism though, we are seeking for the manifesting of Enlightenment in our lives. The great promise in the Lotus Sutra, by the Buddha, is that through this teaching we can all attain the same enlightenment as all Buddhas.

As we make the causes today, which will set a precedence for the coming year, let us not do as the elders of the Sangha did, and default to our past patterns of behaviors. Let us not just settle for whatever life throw our way. Instead, we can choose to focus on being ready to attain enlightenment, chanting Odaimoku and reciting the Sutra.

Making this determination, and following through to the best of our ability let us make a pledge that a year from now we can proclaim, just as the elders of the Buddha's Sangha did;

> *"Today we are not what we were then. We have obtained*
> *what we did not expect*
> *to obtain just as the poor son obtained the*
> *innumerable treasures." (Lotus Sutra, Chapter IV)*

Namu Myoho Renge Kyo!
Happy New Year 2012

Continued Unrelenting Effort

Continued Unrelenting Effort – June 16, 2012 Meditation

Every once in a while it is nice to have a relaxing day with nothing to do, no schedule, no alarms, no meeting, just nothing but lounging around reading or watching movies or snaking and napping. For some people those moments never really arrive, it is as if they are a mirage on the shimmering horizon. For others, even when they arrive they aren't what they imagined they were or they are completely missed.

In Buddhism there is no great taskmaster goading us ever onward day after day, though some perhaps practice with a compulsion that makes it seem as though there is. Our practice allows us to take all the breaks we wish, relax all we can or even completely quit for a while. There is no one standing behind us urging us on, keeping tally, or punishing us for not doing something. It just doesn't work that way.

And yet in spite of such an easy schedule the actual work of changing ourselves never goes away, it's always there. The task can get ever bigger if in our laziness we continue with old patterns of behavior and make poor choices, which of course we hope doesn't happen. Sometimes we may wish that somehow magically all the work of changing our lives can be done with out any effort. Sometimes we may think we have finished our self-work, that we have achieved a certain level which we are satisfied with.

> *"At that time I thought that I had attained extinction. But now I know that the extinction I attained is not the true one." (Lotus Sutra, Chapter III)*

The proof of the pudding in Buddhism is not so much a matter of our intellectual assessment of personal results as it is the observation of the results in our lives and the lives of those around us. It isn't a matter of our coming to some conclusion that we have achieved some state in our Buddhist practice. The proof is in how our life is manifesting and whether our interactions with our environment and society are ones of positive results.

> *"Those Bodhisattvas will not have just begun to aspire for enlightenment. A long time before that they will have already planted the roots of virtue, performed the brahma practices under many hundreds of thousands of billions of Buddhas, received the praises of the Buddhas, studied the wisdom of the Buddhas, obtained great supernatural powers, and understood all the teachings of the Buddhas. They will he upright, honest, and resolute in mind. The world of that Buddha will be filled with such Bodhisattvas." (Lotus Sutra, Chapter III)*

Our work of study and practice can never in all honesty ever really be done. To become satisfied with our accomplishments is a delusion just as it is to feel guilty over our lack of accomplishments is also a delusion. Our

Buddhist practice is not one of just self, it includes others as well. Our own accomplishments are nothing without equally benefiting our society.

> *"The Buddhas, the World-Honored Ones, expound the Dharma with expedients, that is, with various stories of previous lives, with various parables, with various similes, and with various discourses only for the purpose of causing all living beings to attain Anuttara-samyak-sambodhi." (Lotus Sutra, Chapter III)*

I hope you see that our labor, our effort to become enlightened is not an impossible burden to weigh us down. Because we make effort, even small effort, the load becomes lighter. The accumulation of efforts over days, weeks, and years, actually makes the work not only easier to manage but lighter as well. Do not become discouraged because you think you have not done much or can only do little, every effort no matter how seemingly insignificant is really a great effort compared to no effort. Let it be a labor of love for yourself and for others.

Comfort For Others – March 26, 2012 Meditation

Yesterday I began what will be a few days of looking into how we can benefit others, how we can turn the self-work we do outward. Our own enlightenment can not occur outside the context of the people we interact with. Plus we have that first Bodhisattva vow thingy to consider, you know, helping others to attain enlightenment even before ourselves. Tricky that.

Appreciation, genuine and sincere, for other people is an important practice. Remember it isn't that someone does something for us and we thank them, although that we should definitely practice. The kind of appreciation we can try to practice is an expression of the value of their very existence, their presence in our life, good or bad. Regardless of the energy they bring us, they allow us to change to grow and to practice the Bodhisattva way.

Here's the sticky wicket, though, if there is one. We need to do so honestly and genuinely. It doesn't work quite as well and it isn't quite as connecting if it is mere formality. Here are some suggestions; give comfort without lying, smile without hesitation, give without expectation, and guide without misleading.

Now that's a lot of stuff to do. I'll probably need to remind myself about these later on. But for now it does give us some things to work on. They are not impossible, but they may be unfamiliar. That's alright, we're just trying things one step at a time, little by little.

> *"He fastened a priceless gem inside the garment of the man as a gift to him, and went out." (Lotus Sutra, Chapter VIII)*

I think, as I look at the list, perhaps the hardest thing to do is to give without expectation. For you it may be something else. But to sustain appreciation and generosity takes a great deal of effort and it is hard to do that when there is no reciprocation or recognition. Very, very, hard.

> *"The drunken man did not notice what his friend had given him." (Lotus Sutra, Chapter VIII)*

But keeping in mind that the other person may not be aware of or able to receive your efforts. Perhaps they are suffering so greatly and they are not used to someone being kind. Or maybe the only kindness they have experienced was a ploy to use them.

> *"The gem is still there, and you do not notice it. You are working hard, and worrying about your livelihood. What a fool you are! Trade that gem for what you want! You will not be short of anything you want." (Lotus Sutra, Chapter VIII)*

One Step At A Time – April 23, 2012

It has been four months since I started writing these daily meditations. This isn't a particularly long time yet it is a milestone, since I wasn't sure I would be able to continue this for even a month or so. It was my determination , and still is, to do this for a year.

There have been times when writing these has been difficult either due to time or lack of what seem like fresh or worthy ideas. Sometimes I am able to write a few days in advance and sometimes I am writing them the night before they actually post.

This idea of having a goal and then looking at it almost as if 'well that's a good idea but I'm not sure I can do it' is kind of fascinating. There is the aspect of making ourselves open to first thinking of doing something. Then we need to think of something that is beyond what we are currently doing, otherwise there is no growth. Then we need to try not to be discouraged by what may seem impossible and keep on doing it.

Our practice mirrors this in many ways. When we practice we formulate an idea of improving our lives. We begin to be aware of possibilities we did not know existed. We open our minds up to considering changes that previously we would not have even considered.

Our continued practice gives us a framework around which we can take concrete measures to achieving our goal. So, we have a goal, we have a plan and next we need to get it all done.

The getting it done part is hard, especially when we want so bad to achieve our goal. It can be difficult to look at our lives as actually changing when we only look at them from the perspective of one day at a time. Sometimes the distance between formulation of goal and achieving the goal can seem impossibly long.

Daily we may not see any change but gradually over time an accumulation of little changes mounts up to be a dramatic and noticeable change. It is hard to have the patience to be patient.

> *"Hell, the region of hungry spirits, and the region of animals, that is, the three evil regions will be eliminated. The sufferings of birth, old age, disease and death will gradually be eliminated." (Lotus Sutra, ChapterXXV)*

The four month accomplishment of writing these daily meditations began with a single post and it is by the accumulation of single posts that 120 are written. Day by day continue to make effort to eliminate the sufferings from your life so that gradually you can accumulate the joys of enlightenment in your life.

Not Easy – August 3, 2012 Meditation

Working on the 35 Day Practice guide was a great activity for me, as I hope it was for anyone who kept up with it. It was a good opportunity for me to look at the Lotus Sutra from what I imagine a new person would view it. It isn't easy to begin to practice Buddhism and the Lotus Sutra, it is sometimes even harder to keep on going for many years.

The challenges of practice are many, they sometimes include family, friends, society, job, finances, time, perceptions of self and many more, probably as many different reasons as there are people who practice. We may all secretly harbor a wish for an easy time of practice, even possibly an easy comfortable practice.

> *"Needless to say, those who keep all the passages of this sutra and make various offerings to this sutra are great Bodhisattvas. Medicine-King, know this! They should be considered to have given up the rewards of their pure karmas and appeared in the evil world after my extinction in order to expound this sutra out of their compassion towards all living beings." (Lotus Sutra, Chapter X)*

We should always keep in our mind that fundamentally our reason for practicing Buddhism is because we wish to save other beings, and we gave up lives of ease and comfort so that we could expound this Sutra in the age after the death of the Buddha. This is a pretty powerful statement, and of course it relies upon a certain belief in cause and effect and the truth of the words of the Buddha.

We have to ask ourselves though, if we don't fully believe in these words, by what cause have we come into contact with the Lotus Sutra? What is our relationship with the Lotus Sutra? We can easily say that it is merely a chance encounter in this life of seemingly unlimited chance encounters. But even if it is a chance encounter we still must have a connection because who else is attempting to practice the Lotus Sutra in this age after the death of the Buddha.

> *"The good men or women who expound even a phrase of the Sutra of the Lotus Flower of the Wonderful Dharma even to one person even in secret after my extinction, know this, are my messengers. They are dispatched by me. They do my work." (Lotus Sutra, Chapter X)*

If you are such a person who practices, to any degree, the teachings of the Lotus Sutra then you are in fact fulfilling a promise, which originally was to practice at this time. No matter how seemingly insignificant you may view your actions or practice the Buddha is very clear that you are functioning in fact, even if not yet in belief, as a messenger of the Buddha.

I encourage each of us to deeply consider our wonderful karmic connection to the Lotus Sutra. The deeper we can absorb this into our lives, the deeper we relate to this, the greater our joy and the greater our merit. Yet even a moment of practice in this age is greater than all the practices performed during the lifetime of the Buddha.

Yes, it is that hard! So you should be proud of your great efforts and continue your practice no matter what.

"If you wish to obtain quickly the knowledge of the equality and differences of all things, keep this sutra, and also make offerings to the keeper of this sutra! Anyone who keeps the Sutra of the Lotus Flower of the Wonderful Dharma, know this, has compassion towards all living beings because he is my messenger. Anyone who keeps The Sutra of the Lotus Flower of the Wonderful Dharma should be considered to have given up his pure world and come here out of his compassion towards all living beings. Know that he can appear wherever he wishes! He should be considered to have appeared in this evil world in order to expound the unsurpassed Dharma." (Lotus Sutra, Chapter X)

No Escape

No Escape – October 2, 2012 Meditation

Have you ever had a dog mix it up with a skunk?

Well, the thing is when a dog and a skunk mix it up the dog probably comes out worse off. No matter what the poor thing does it can't escape the smell and if the dog comes into the house you can't either.

As we live our life we are continually making causes in response to effects we are experiencing. While it may seem sometimes like we can get away with making causes and receive no effect, either good or bad, in reality we can not escape unaffected.

We don't try to make good causes and avoid making bad ones because some one will punish us, instead we do so because it is the surest way for us to positively control the elimination of suffering in our lives.

> *"Some living beings planted the roots of good in their previous existence. Some of the roots have fully developed." (Lotus Sutra, Chapter IV)*

On one level our previous existence was only a moment ago. Chanting Namu Myoho Renge Kyo is the surest way to ensure not just the planting of good roots, but also of nourishing what has been planted.

Mirrors

Mirrors – May 8, 2012 Meditation

I was driving home from my road trip through the New England states and I heard a song on the radio which really impressed me. The title of the song is No Mirrors In My Nana's House by Ysaye Maria Barnwell. The song is about a young girl growing up in her grandmother's house where there were no mirrors.

Every day the girl saw the beauty in her grandmother's eyes. She never knew that her skin was too dark, or her clothes didn't fit. The young girl only knew herself through the beauty her grandmother saw in her.

Imagine your life if you did not see in the mirror every day the faults we see that limit our joy. Imagine if you didn't see yourself as too fat, or too skinny, or too poor, or not pretty, or not stylish enough. Imagine if you only saw the beauty that is at the depths of your life. Imagine if you could see first the Buddha in your life before you saw all the little things we normally use to judge ourselves by.

> *"Although he has not yet obtained the wonderful body of the Bodhisattva who knows the nature of the Dharma without-asravas, he will be able to have all these things reflected on his pure and natural body."*
> *(Lotus Sutra, Chapter XIX)*

Whether we can see it or not and whether or not we think it is there, our life already reflects, it already manifests the life of the Buddha. But it is possible for us to tell ourselves, to convince ourselves that we are not as we truly are.

We see the distortions reflected back to us via the mirror of society and are unable to see ourselves reflected in the mirror of Buddhism.

In Nichiren Buddhism we talk about polishing our mirror. The mirror we are trying to polish is the mirror that most truly reflects our Buddha life. When we are deceived by false images of ourselves we are misled into thinking that we are not worthy or incapable of manifesting such a great and wondrous thing as enlightenment.

> *"Just as a reflection is seen in a clear mirror, all things in the world will be reflected on the pure body of this person, that is, of this Bodhisattva. No one but he will be able to see all things clearly."*
> *(Lotus Sutra, Chapter XIX)*

Chant every day so that the true mirror of enlightenment is clear and you can see the Buddha reflected back to you as you look at yourself.

Faith As A Bargain – August 15, 2012 Meditation

The bargain goes something like this; if I am good, if I obey all the rules, I do everything required of me, then life will be good and I'll be treated fairly. For some that is the definition of faith, a faith based upon a wish for security. A faith founded on an attempt to manipulate reality, an attempt to strike a bargain which ultimately does not come true because the bargain was made by only one person – ourselves.

> *"It is difficult to keep this sutra after my extinction.*
> *Since I attained the enlightenment of the Buddha,*
> *I have expounded many sutras in innumerable*
> *worlds. This sutra is the most excellent. To keep*
> *this sutra is to keep me." (Lotus Sutra, Chapter XI)*

We know from the outset that it will be hard to keep this sutra. Yet how do we approach this faith, this practice without entering into some kind of bargain? We know that we are guaranteed to attain enlightenment if we keep faith in, practice, study and teach this Lotus Sutra. Isn't that some kind of bargain?

> *"We will wear the armor of endurance because we*
> *respect and believe you. We will endure all these*

difficulties in order to expound this sutra." (Lotus Sutra, Chapter XII)

When we think about the benefit of enlightenment it has been my experience that many people think this is some magic point in life when trouble cease to occur. Another common misunderstanding is that somehow our enlightenment will be like some person sitting peacefully under a tree meditating endlessly, a life of bliss and ease.

Enlightenment though is not like that. That moment in time, which we so famously admire, was merely an awakening a moment in the life of the Buddha. From that point on the Buddha worked tirelessly and without comfort, to spread the awakening he experienced. I wonder how many people have that as their image?

Going to the first of the Bodhisattva vows, and from the quote above we see that we do all of this so that we will be able to lead others to the same awakening.

If we remain stuck in the kind of faith that is based upon the bargain, a faith that comes with a contract we present as a demand, then we ignore all the teachings of all the Buddhas in all the Sutras. We are in essence trying to impose our control on the life without regard to the truth or fundamental reality.

This kind of bargain is certain to eventually crumble. When that occurs we will be presented with a golden moment, a moment where we can proceed with a faith founded on our experiences and one that leads us to a true belief in Buddhism, and not as I mentioned previously a belief in the concept of Buddhism.

"Anyone who understands why the Buddhas expound many sutras, who knows the position of this sutra in the series of sutras, and who expounds it after my extinction according to its true meaning, will be able to eliminate the darkness of the living beings of the world where he walks about, just as the light of the sun and the moon eliminates all darkness, he will be able to cause innumerable Bodhisattvas to dwell finally in the One Vehicle."
(Lotus Sutra, Chapter XXI)

Ever Deepening

Ever Deepening – April 19, 2012 Meditation

Occasionally I am asked questions such as how long will it take me to become enlightened, or if I practice a certain length of time will I be enlightened. Usually these questions come from people not familiar with Buddhism, but sometimes they do come from practitioners. And if it isn't a question similar to those it is some statement that indicates there is a belief that enlightenment is a terminus point.

I usually respond with something to the effect that there is no there there. However, I ran across this quote which perhaps says what I am trying to express much more eloquently.

> *"Enlightenment is not a peak experience. It's a permanent shift in paradigm that deepens day by day." (Shinzen Young)*

You see it is not a destination we are looking towards reaching it is an accumulated change in the way we live, the way we experience and manifest our lives. It isn't an accumulation of knowledge but an accumulated experience of incorporating wisdom and life lessons into our daily existence and then living in such a way continually manifesting those lessons.

"That Buddha will appear in his world at first as a prince. The prince will give up his princeship and worldly fame. He will renounce the world at the end of his life as a layman, and attain the enlightenment of the Buddha." (Lotus Sutra, Chapter III)

I believe that it is somewhat misleading, the words we use, such as attain enlightenment. Perhaps I am wrong but I believe that the attainment is a actually a process and not the statement of the result. What actually occurs I believe is the attainment is an awakening to the truth that we all possess Buddha within, though we also possess other conditions as well.

"All of you will be able to attain the enlightenment of the Buddha if you believe and receive these words of mine." (Lotus Sutra, Chapter III)

It is through out belief a belief that says I understand what I must do, I understand where I must begin. We cultivate a belief that is based not upon an unknowable thing but a belief that is based upon an awareness of the truth of Buddha existing within our very lives.

Awakening to this and nurturing this belief we revere the teachings of the Buddha and begin to apply them ever increasing deeper.

"Those who seek the enlightenment of the Buddha are as various as previously stated. A kalpa will not be long enough to describe the variety of them. They will be able to understand [this sutra] by faith. Expound to them the Sutra of the Lotus Flower of the Wonderful Dharma!" (Lotus Sutra, Chapter III)

Equality

Equality – April 2, 2012 Meditation

> *"After the game the king and pawn go into the same box." (Italian proverb)*

Many words are used to describe the differences we see in others and even in ourselves. We attribute value descriptors so freely I wonder if sometimes we are even aware. We say things like 'they are…', 'he is….', and 'I am…'

In all instances these are not necessarily the beginning of comparison statements, though frequently there is an implied comparison; even if the comparison is in the positive it still exists.

> *"My treasures are limitless. I should not give inferior, smaller carts to them. They are all my children. Therefore, I love them without partiality. I have a countless number of these large carts of the seven treasures. I gave one of these to each of my children equally. There should be no discrimination." (Lotus Sutra, Chapter III)*

The Lotus Sutra is very clear on the concept of non-discrimination and equality. There really is no permanently existing basis of differences.

On the surface, yes we observe variations, however there is nothing on which to base a value of greater or lesser superiority.

> *"I see all living beings equally. I have no partiality for them. There is not 'this one' or 'that one' to me. I transcend love and hatred. I am attached to nothing. I am hindered by nothing. I always expound the Dharma to all living beings equally. I expound the Dharma to many in the same way as to one." (Lotus Sutra, Chapter V)*

My original thought when I began writing was motivated by recent efforts in North Carolina, USA to further put into law a strengthening of a discrimination that currently exists regarding the right of people to love and be with whom they choose.

As I began writing I still held that thought, however I keep coming back to the idea of internalized inequality. By this I mean the comparisons we impose upon ourselves. How often do we, you and I, hold onto and incorporate into our beliefs the idea that we are either not good enough or that we are incapable of becoming enlightened?

Yet, from a Buddhist perspective this is not true nor is it fundamentally possible.

> *"Excellent, excellent! You, Sakyamuni, the World-Honored One, have expounded to this great multitude the Sutra of the Lotus Flower of the Wonderful Dharma, the Teaching of Equality, the Great Wisdom, the Dharma for Bodhisattvas, the Dharma Upheld by the Buddhas. So it is, so it is.*

What you, Sakyamuni, the World-Honored One,
have expounded is all true." (Lotus Sutra, Chapter
XI)

It isn't easy to abandon the messages of inequality, to turn
aside from them and believe and practice equality. It isn't
easy to do this when relating to others in our environment,
it isn't easy to do this when relating to ourselves. We
can continue to try and exert ourselves in practicing the
Wonderful Dharma of the Lotus Flower Sutra.

As Nichiren says in the Sho Jiso Sho;

"Endeavor! Endeavor, to strengthen your faith!"

Effective Giving – April 16, 2012 Meditation

The other day a good friend of mine, Rabbi Jonathan F. posted the following on his Twitter feed:

> *"An effective gift comes from insight into another's actual needs" Meditation for 7th Day of Omer (13 August 2012)*

https://twitter.com/rabbijonathan/
status/190965768651939842

How do we approach the idea of giving a gift that considers the other's actual needs?

Within the Lotus Sutra there are five practices that are given to us; keep, read, recite, copy, and expound.

Let us consider the practice of expounding, and do so from the perspective that "comes from the insight into another's actual needs."

> *"To those who were seeking Sravakahood, he expounded the teaching of the four truths, a teaching suitable for them, saved them from birth, old age, disease, and death, and caused them to attain Nirvana. To those who were seeking*

Pratyekabuddhahood, he expounded the teaching
of the twelve causes, a teaching suitable for them.
To Bodhisattvas, he expounded the teaching of the
six paramitas, a teaching suitable for them, and
caused them to attain Anuttara-samyak-sambodhi,
that is, to obtain the knowledge of the equality and
differences of all things." (Lotus Sutra, Chapter I)

Previous to the Lotus Sutra the Buddha expounded the
teachings that were suitable to various types of people. If
we look at this in a superficial way it may seem that he was
teaching to the needs of each individual. We might be able
to justify this thinking if it were not for the later teachings
contained in the Lotus Sutra.

As we learn in Chapter II and beyond, prior to the Lotus
Sutra, the Buddha was not in fact teaching according to the
actual needs of those individuals. He was only teaching
according to each person's desires, or what they wanted to
hear.

"As a rule, the World-Honored Ones expound the
true teaching only after a long period of expounding
expedient teachings." (Lotus Sutra, Chapter II)

We know that the teaching contained in the Lotus Sutra
is not simply a replacement for previous teachings, it is
actually a further extension of those teachings. Where
those previous teaching left off is where the Lotus Sutra
begins.

So how does this apply to our practice of 'expounding' the
Lotus Sutra?

"When you see anyone who does not receive this sutra by faith, you should show him some other profound teachings of mine, teach him, benefit him, and cause him to rejoice. When you do all this, you will be able to repay the favors given to you by the Buddhas." (Lotus Sutra, Chapter XXII)

Sharing and teaching others about Buddhism, I believe, must first come from the desire to benefit the other person, not a personal desire to have 'accomplished' some conversion act.

If we think about the parable of the Burning House, the father does not carry out, 'force conversion', the children from the sufferings in the house. Instead he encourages them, he shows them the alternatives available. If he had carried them out one by one he would not have been able to save them all. But by presenting them with a choice of carts, by showing them the joy of Buddhism they all came running out and all were saved.

We may be able to cleverly bend someone's will, or coerce, or cajole someone into practicing Buddhism. Our clever words may move some, but it is our actions to benefit others that will most effectively show others the truth of Buddhism.

If a person is not interested in Buddhism, then we need not worry. We can cause them to praise the Buddha and create the causes for future lifetimes if we can cause them to have great joy! If they praise your behavior and your life, then they are offering praise to the Buddha.

Dreaming

Dreaming – June 19, 2012 Meditation

I am not sure if you can remember back to your childhood or to high school and recall what your dreams or aspirations were. I know that I can not. Some of my oldest memories of hopes and dreams are from the time both shortly before and after I became Buddhist.

> "I never dreamed of having this store of treasures myself. It has come to me unexpectedly." (Lotus Sutra, Chapter IV)

My dreams before I ran into an active Sangha were merely to survive the Marine Corps and Vietnam and to somehow find a way to put the philosophy of Buddhism into practice. That wish was fulfilled one evening while I was stationed in Memphis, TN way back in 1969. Sometime after that I recall having the dream or hope to become a priest. It took much longer to realize my goal of becoming a priest.

I can recall my first night when I received my Omandala. I felt so excited, so happy, so a peace, and so confident that my life would be one of joy. Of course I didn't really understand what I had just done, receiving my Omandala, but it connected with me in a very profound way.

I think what I didn't realize is that the desire for enlightenment had been aroused within my life. I did know that there was something that had happened when I first began learning about the Lotus Sutra.

A few years ago I was talking with a Japanese priest and he asked me if I thought that the Lotus Sutra was strange to Americans. I wasn't sure how to answer this, as I knew from my own experience that it just seemed natural. He went on to ask if religions like Mormon or Jehovah's Witness or some of the Pentecostal religions were strange? I said that to some people they are considered strange. He said that what I felt when I was first exposed to the Lotus Sutra was an awakening within my life to a connection to this great teaching. He said that what we need to realize when we propagate Nichiren Buddhism is that we are not really asking people to change their beliefs so much as awaken them to the truth, to the Lotus Sutra that exists at the core of their lives.

> *"I attained the truth of the reality of all things. I am now in deep dhyana-concentration. I see the Buddhas of the worlds of the ten quarters." (Lotus Sutra, Chapter XIV)*

As you think about your dreams, your goals, your aspirations consider the role the Lotus Sutra can and does play in your life even if you are at times unaware. Consider the fundamental truths of things like cause and effect, 10 Worlds, equality of all beings and so forth. Faith in the Lotus Sutra isn't so much a belief in what isn't apparent, as it is an awakening to the truths taught.

"I have already expounded to you the truth of the reality of all things." (Lotus Sutra, Chapter II)

Remember our fundamental dream or aspiration is for enlightenment.

Going Slowly – August 2, 2012 Meditation

Imagine this if you will. You are driving down the road and in your car is a very fragile load, let's say you have a crock-pot full of stew, some trays of food and you are on your way to a potluck supper. You want your items to arrive un-spilled and in good shape so that everyone will enjoy your contribution.

As you drive you navigate the turns slowly, so you don't spill anything, and you drive with great caution making sure you have plenty of time to stop if you need to without slamming on the brakes. You notice that people are whizzing around you when they can, even though you are driving close to the speed limit. The speed limit by the way is not necessarily the speed at which you must drive it is in stead the maximum speed you should drive.

Still, the other drivers you sense are irritated at your slow and cautious pace.

You know why you are driving with such great caution, the other drivers, however, do not. Imagine if they did know, do you think they might be as irritated or impatient?

How many times do we become irritated when someone isn't going as fast as we think they should, or who isn't performing according to our standards? Are we like these drivers in our fictitious story? Do we take the time to consider there might be extenuating circumstances why someone is not doing things in a way to meet our expectations?

It is easy to judge other people and their actions without considering. It is not easy to always be gracious and kind. It is easy to construct a story about the other person being slow, stupid, or incompetent. It is not easy to remember that we do not fully understand all the circumstances in their lives.

> *"When we heard your first teaching, we did not know that that teaching was an expedient one expounded according to our capacities. Therefore, we believed and received that teaching at once, thought it over, and attained the enlightenment to be attained by that teaching." (Lotus Sutra, Chapter III)*

The Buddha's first disciples were guilty of making a false assumption it is only with the teaching and their participation in the Lotus Sutra that they were able to learn the truth the Buddha only alluded to in his early teachings.

So too, when we mistakenly make assumptions of others we miss the truth of their lives. This causes us suffering as well as potentially causing others suffering. We suffer when we think less of others or do not regard their lives and their inherent Buddha. We also diminish their lives and do not offer them the cause to awaken to enlightenment.

Our daily relationships, no matter how brief or fleeting, are opportunities to not only practice Buddhism but to allow others to connect with the Lotus Sutra. It isn't just what we say with our mouths it is what we hold in our hearts.

"The extinction of suffering is called the third truth. In order to attain this extinction, the eight right ways must be practiced. Freedom from the bonds of suffering, that is, from illusions is called emancipation." (Lotus Sutra, Chapter III)

Getting To Know God – August 10, 2012 Meditation

*"A man goes to a monastery and asks the head
monk there, Father Frederick, to help him find
God. The Father instructs the man to touch his
nose every day exactly at ten o'clock in the morning
and at three o'clock in the afternoon. He was not
to touch it earlier or later, only exactly at the times
specified. It turns out the man frequently would
remember either too early or too late, and often
would not remember at all. Sometimes he would
remember one time but forget the other. What the
man eventually realized that it is hard enough to
make change happen much less spiritual change. It
is difficult enough to make spiritual change however
it is even harder to remember to make the effort."
Paraphrased from* The Five Stages of The Soul *by
Harry R. Moody and David Carroll*

What this story teaches us is perhaps somewhat self-evident
yet worth contemplating. In the Eightfold Path we have
Right Effort, Right Intention. It is easy to have an intention
for something to happen in our lives, it is sometime more
problematic to couple the intention with the effort.

Our lives are strongly influenced by our habitual way
of living. We may not even realize the trap we are in
until we try to engage in something so intentional as the

seemingly simple act of touching our noses twice a day at very specified times. Of course you might think setting a timer, say on your pocket phone or computer, could solve the problem. But that is a habitual response, looking for an easy way to accomplish what has been already admitted by thinking this way, that doing it might be beyond your realm of possibility.

Touching one's nose is not a very complicated activity even within the limitations prescribed; imagine how much more complicated it is to change our patterns of behavior. For some even doing morning and evening prayers is challenging, as we try to fit it into our already busy lives instead of fitting our busy lives into our prayers.

> *"Anyone who, while he is seeking the enlightenment of the Buddha, sees or hears this Sutra of the Lotus Flower of the Wonderful Dharma, and after hearing it, understands it by faith and keeps it, know this, will approach Anuttara-samyak- sambodhi." (Lotus Sutra, Chapter X)*

> *"I made a vow to attain unsurpassed Bodhi. I never faltered in seeking it. I practiced almsgiving in order to complete the six paramitas. I never grudged elephants, horses, the seven treasures, countries, cities, wives, children, menservants, maidservants or attendants. I did not spare my head, eyes, marrow, brain, flesh, hands or feet. I did not spare even my life." (Lotus Sutra, Chapter XII)*

While it is true, as it says in the Lotus Sutra, we can gain immeasurable merits from merely associating with the Lotus Sutra, the ultimate purpose of Buddhist practice come from our dedicated efforts to practice and strive in living the Lotus Sutra.

Flowers

Flowers – April 3, 2012 Meditation

Happy Birthday U.(name omitted)!

> *"She is eloquent without hindrance. She is compassionate towards all living beings just as a mother is towards her babe. She obtained all merits. Her thoughts and words are wonderful and great. She is compassionate, humble, gentle and graceful. She has already been qualified to attain Bodhi, and to become a Buddha quickly"* (Lotus Sutra, Chapter XII)

It might be said that if someone says nice things but doesn't mean it they are like a flower with no scent. And while the smell emitted by a flower follows the wind a person's reputation will spread far and wide regardless of which way the wind blows.

Eventually the insincere person is revealed, either by adverse circumstances or ill fortune, or some tragedy either to themselves or to those they have been false to.

> *"I hear your gentle voice. Your voice is deep and wonderful. You expound the Pure Dharma. My heart is filled with great joy. All my doubts are gone. I have obtained true wisdom."* (Lotus Sutra, Chapter III)

45

It is said numerous times in the Lotus Sutra that the Buddha has a golden pure voice and that what he has taught is all true. In response fragrant flowers rained down from the heavens.

Let us make strenuous efforts to practice with a wonderful voice pure and golden.

We may say things we wish we had not, we may say harsh things, or speak in anger, even though our mind says we should not. You may berate yourself and become angry with yourself. In a way you are doing the same thing to yourself that you did to the other. Further you are in fact strengthening your negative energy.

Be kind to yourself, smile at this negative energy. Remember be sincere to yourself. Recognize what you have done be mindful of this. Continue doing this and you will become more aware of those things and moments in which you respond in ways you do not wish to. Then you can begin to practice new responses more in keeping with your Buddhist beliefs. Mindfulness starts with yourself.

Uttering golden and pure words to others begins with you. Let the fragrant mandarava flowers appear in your life.

> *"In reality this world of mine is peaceful. It is filled with gods and men. The gardens, forests, and stately buildings are adorned with various treasures; the jeweled trees have many flowers and fruits; the living beings are enjoying themselves; and the gods are beating heavenly drums making various kinds of music, and raining mandarava-flowers on the great multitude and me." (Lotus Sutra, Chapter XVI)*

False Assumptions

False Assumptions – April 24, 2012 Meditation

Four people are flying in an airplane, the pilot, a professor, a hiker and another individual. The plane begins to have problems and it become apparent that it will crash. So the pilot announces that there are only three parachutes and that he is going to take one of them. The professor says that since he is so important and brilliant he will take another. The hiker then turns to the other person and says there are still two chutes left, because the professor in all of his brilliance grabbed the hiker's backpack.

As we go through life how often do we act like the professor, thinking that we have everything figured out? If you are anything like me, perhaps great portions of your life are lived that way, all the way up until something goes wrong. It is easy to go through life thinking that we have all the answers and everything is planned out.

I work in a hospital, visiting people who are sick and even dying. Often people share how unexpected their illness was or impending death is. We go through life planning all sorts of things, frequently based upon the faulty assumption that we are in control.

Sometimes we fail to consider that the most effective plan we can make is the important activity of practicing

Buddhism. We can with no certainty predict what the future will be like, even if we live each day with the attitude that we are somehow in control. The most effective thing for our future is the day-to-day practice of Buddhism.

> *"It is because, if they see me for a long time, they will not plant the roots of good, but become poor and base, and cling to the five desires so much that they will he caught in the nets of wrong views."*
> *(Lotus Sutra, Chapter XVI)*

We are in a sense lulled into a false sense of security by the seemingly predictable events of our lives. It is because of this false sense of security, the predictability of the day to day, that we fail to notice the importance of engaging in the one practice that can afford us with the real security of the elimination of suffering.

It is important to note though, that eliminating suffering is not the same as having no problems.

There are time, for certain, that we will experience difficulties in our lives, and while a back pack is important the greatest thing to possess is the parachute.

> *"The roots of good which they have planted will help them aspire for unsurpassed enlightenment."*
> *(Lotus Sutra, Chapter XVII)*

FOMO

FOMO – April 10, 2012 Meditation

Two days ago I wrote about the purpose of the appearance of Buddhas. That being to cause all people to seek enlightenment and to show them the way to do so. At the conclusion I proposed the question, 'why do we practice the Buddha's teachings?'

Yesterday (link: http://myoshoji.org/blog/index.php/archives/2399) I wrote about how easy it is to become distracted and abandon our practice, how most people it seems do so. Possibly because it is too hard to practice Buddhism, or because they do not keep in their hearts their original intent.

The 'Fear of Missing Out' FOMO is characterized by the inability to say no to things that pop up in our lives. It is manifest in an almost compulsive need to be involved in doing something, even if distracting, for fear that we may be missing some thing. The cell phone is a good example; how easy is it for you to avoid rushing to pick up the phone on the first or second ring? What kind of need is seeking to be fulfilled by checking email constantly?

One of the symptoms of this is being unfocused and stressed out. Another is being overwhelmed.

"Exert yourselves and concentrate your minds!
Now I will tell you about this matter.
Do not doubt me! My wisdom is difficult to
understand. Arouse your power of faith,
And do good patiently! You will be able to hear the
Dharma that you have never heard before." (Lotus
Sutra, Chapter XV)

It is easy to become distracted from our Buddhist practice.
There are many things that compete for our time and
attention. Some of those things can really nag at us, sort of
like the little icon on your phone or computer that tells you
there are X number of emails waiting your viewing.

Unfortunately, in Buddhism there isn't a little nag icon
that pops up to remind you of the importance of practice
and study, though you can probably find an app for it (link:
http://timelessremindersblog.com/).

"All of you should concentrate your minds, wear
the armor of endeavors, and be resolute." (Lotus
Sutra, Chapter XV)

This is actually part of the practice of Buddhism, being
self-motivated. We need to continually examine our lives,
looking for the things that hinder us in our practice as well
as in becoming enlightened.

"He should always make it a pleasure to sit in
dhyana. He should live in a retired place and
concentrate his mind. Manjusri! A retired place is
the first thing he should approach." (Lotus Sutra,
Chapter XIV)

I think for us today, that retired place is learning to be comfortable with letting the nag-icon go unattended, with peace, ease and comfort, when it is time to engage in our practice. Let go of your FOMO 'fear of missing out'.

Fourteen

Fourteen – January 14, 2012 Meditation

> "I have reigned more than fifty years in victory
> and peace," the great caliph Abdul Rahim once
> remarked. "During this time I have been beloved
> by my people, dreaded by my enemies, and
> respected by my allies. Riches and honors, power
> and pleasure have all been at my beck and call, nor
> has any earthly pleasure been missing to complete
> my sense of perfect bliss. In this situation I have
> diligently numbered the days of pure and genuine
> happiness that have fallen to my lot. They number
> fourteen." (Harry Moody & David Carroll, The Five
> Stages of the Soul; p. 5)

Just fourteen days? Wow, there goes the myth that money
and power can make you happy. What is it that makes us
happy, and more importantly, what is happiness?

How much have we thought about what happiness really
is? We all probably have at one time or another thought to
ourselves that we are not presently happy. But do we even
know what would make us happy?

Maybe there is a nagging voice inside your head that asks:
'Is this all there is? Is this as good as it gets?" A sense of
dissatisfaction may pervade our thinking and feelings, but

have we really deeply considered what is the source of that dissatisfaction or disquiet?

> "Just as a torch dispels darkness, this Sutra of the
> Lotus Flower of the Wonderful Dharma saves all
> living beings from all sufferings, from all diseases,
> and from all the bonds of birth and death. The
> merits to be given to the person who, after hearing
> this Sutra of the Lotus Flower of the Wonderful
> Dharma, copies it, or causes others to copy it,
> cannot be measured even by the wisdom of the
> Buddha." (Lotus Sutra, Chapter XXII)

We may not realize the gradual lightening of our delusional self, but from the very first moment we contact the Lotus Sutra a change is taking place within our lives. It doesn't matter how long a cave has been dark, thousands of years even, yet a single moment of light from any source instantly removes the darkness.

> "Therefore, the man of wisdom
> who hears the benefits of these merits
> and who keeps this sutra after my extinction, will
> be able to attain the enlightenment of the Buddha
> definitely and doubtlessly." (Lotus Sutra, Chapter
> XXI)

Matsubagayatsu Commeration

Matsubagayatsu Persecution Commemoration - August 25, 2019

(Dedicated to members practicing in Argentina)

Today, the day I am writing this, is August 27, 2019, the anniversary of the Matsubagayatsu persecution endured by Nichiren Shonin. It was during this event when thousands of lay believers of the Nembutsu-only school were incited to riot by their clergy with the tacit approval of the government. The incident took place in Kamakura, Japan.

On the evening of the 27th, Nichiren was prompted to leave his dwelling by the urgings of a white monkey. The monkey then led Nichiren up into the hills above his hut. From there it was obvious to Nichiren that if he had ignored the monkey and remained in his hut he most likely would have burned to death or been seriously injured by the rioters.

Frequently when I talk about this event people most often want to focus on the 'miracle' of the intervention of the monkey and Nichiren's escape. While that is certainly interesting, and makes for a good exciting plot line, I don't think it is the most important lesson for us to dwell upon.

What I like to consider is the fortitude of Nichiren, who

was only 39 years old. Surviving the incident is something for us to be thankful for certainly. More important though, I believe, should be our gratitude that after this experience Nichiren continued to preach, teach, and spread the Dharma. If Nichiren had called it quits, even after being rescued by the monkey then it is likely we would not be gathering together and chanting Odaimoku.

For each of us the greater lesson here is not to be discouraged by our obstacles. It is certain that most of our challenges in life will not be resolved by miraculous interventions. Given that fact if we focus on the extraordinary events that allowed Nichiren to survive then we may feel as if the Odaimoku does not benefit us to the degree it did Nichiren. I believe that would be an inaccurate comparison, one that would provide fertile ground for doubt.

The important thing in our lives is to live through our troubles with the same determination and single mindedness that Nichiren exhibited when faced with his own difficulties. Most of us will not face life-threatening persecution for our faith. Some of us may face persecution because we are ass-holes, but few will be persecuted simply because of chanting Odaimoku.

While I have certainly had more than my fair share of extraordinary solutions to my life challenges, most of the time the thing I have gained through chanting is wisdom and courage. Wisdom to be open to solutions I had not previously considered, and courage to persevere even when it may seem hopeless.

I was informed the other day that the members in Argentina were eating only soup because they did not have enough money for food. The economy there is in shambles, inflation is skyrocketing, and food and essentials costs more and more every day. Also wages are stagnant and low, never enough to buy the things needed for basic living.

I can not promise you, or anyone, will see a "white-monkey" appear revealing a solution. Rather I can attest that continuing to uphold your faith, chanting with joy and confidence you can gain the courage to not only endure but thrive in ways you never thought possible.

Notice I said chanting with confidence and great joy. I think this is fundamental. When you can approach your faith, not in desperation, but in true joy and confidence, then an even greater joy wells up within you and even more courage strengthens your resolve.

In my book Contemplating Illness, which is now available in Spanish, I talk about when I first began chanting. At the time I was in the United States Marine Corps and facing some serious challenges from my commanders. I was new in faith, I was young, only 21, I was scared. When I chanted then it was as if I was throwing hand-grenades at the Gohonzon with each Odaimoku. Have you ever chanted with that kind of energy, and desperation? I'm guessing many have.

It isn't wrong to chant that way. It actually normal to an extent. It doesn't mean you doubt the possibilities. You are not weak.

But consider this for a moment. For those who have practiced for a period of time, perhaps you can recall some incidents that have resolved themselves with not much effort or worry. Now when you are faced with something major we think that we need to stress out, tense our muscles, scrub our beads, and scream our heads off. Of course you can do those things, but you don't need to. Rather chant with determination that this will be resolved, find a place in your faith and life that can say, "I don't know how it will work out, but I promise I will continue in my faith until it is resolved, and as I live and practice my faith, I will do so with joy and confidence."

That's hard to do, perhaps sometimes it is the hardest thing to do.

I am praying for your faith and courage, and I pray that your suffering be turned into a wonderful life changing experience which will propel you to enlightenment in this life.

With Gassho,
Kansho Jeffus, Shonin

Treasures We Do Not Seek

Treasures We Do Not Seek – April 20, 2014 Dharma Talk

Good morning thank you for attending the temple this
Easter morning. Even though Easter is not a Buddhist
holiday there is much in the spirit of the holiday we
can appreciate. Today I would like to share with you a
connection I make with one part of the Easter story and the
Lotus Sutra.

As you know I work as a chaplain and in my work here in
Charlotte I am frequently, almost entirely, called to spend
time with Christians. Not being raised in a particularly
Christian family there is really much of the religion I was
not aware of prior to my training to be a chaplain. One of
those things was the idea of Saturday in the story of the
crucifixion and resurrection Christian celebrate at Easter.
Today I would like to talk about Saturday.

In a way the idea of the uncertainty of Saturday after
crucifixion is an appropriate metaphor for many things in
our lives. In case you don't know what I am talking about,
Saturday was a time of great uncertainty for those early
followers of Christ. They had just witnessed their spiritual
teachers death the day before. For my Christian friends
who may read this, please forgive me if I make some
doctrinal errors.

On Saturday those early disciples of Christ who were not yet called Christians were probably very upset, grieving the loss of their teacher just the day before. For us as moderns who know the outcome of the story it is easy to forget how uncertain these people may have felt. They did not know what the future would hold for them. There may have even been the thoughts of giving up, of being spiritually adrift.

In Chapter VI of the Lotus Sutra the arhats say to the Buddha:

> *"We have obtained innumerable treasures although we did not seek them."*

When we read this it is easy to understand both the delight and the acknowledgement of the benefit of the treasure of an improved life condition resulting from our Buddhist practice.

Yet in the time before we see the benefit of our Buddhist faith and practice it isn't easy to be able to claim any delight in benefits not sought after. There are times in our practice when we may face some serious troubles, when moving forward seems terribly hard if not down right impossible.

I imagine Saturday might have been such a time for the followers of Christ. How do you proceed when the worst has happened? How do you go forward after you have lost a loved one? How do you get up the next day after you have been diagnosed with a terminal disease? How do you have a morning cup of coffee when you need to rush to the hospital to be with a sick or dying loved one? How do you find joy when the worst possible thing has happened to you? How do you praise the benefit of the Lotus Sutra when you see no benefit in the moment?

Sometimes it seems our religious beliefs call on us to do the impossible. Yet isn't it really the other way around? When we are faced with the seemingly impossible isn't it our religious or spiritual beliefs the very thing we can rely upon to get us through?

Sometimes we view events as tests of our religion or our faith when really we might better think of it as we have difficulties as a natural part of being alive and religion is what can give us direction in those moments. When you look around at every thing in life think about just how difficult it is to even be alive. Living is a treasure no matter how brief or turbulent it is. Right now there are literally hundreds of dead canker worms on my front porch, there are hundreds more plastered all over the sides of the house. These were living beings that struggled and did not make it. Life is a struggle, but we as humans have an expectation that it will be roses and easy.

We look at resurrection or enlightenment as if this is how every day should be, as if somehow we should expect lives of ease and comfort. We forget too easily the Saturdays of our lives. We forget the years of struggle the Buddha engaged in so he could be awakened. We forget just how tenuous life really is.

Life is the treasure and our awareness of this is the treasure we sometimes are most unaware of and take for granted. This is the first treasure we should celebrate. When we can fully celebrate the treasure of life and realize that Saturday is a key part of that treasure we can be opened to the other treasures in our lives. When we live with a sense of entitlement to lives of ease we delude ourselves and thereby miss the moments of just being alive.

I wish you a joyous day and life as Buddhist, as Christians, as Jews, as Muslims, and as the many other ways of expressing and living as spiritual beings.

September 11 - Fifth Anniversary

Today is September 10, 2006 and tomorrow will be the 11th and the 5th anniversary of the terrorist attacks on the World Trade Center in New York, the Pentagon in Washington, DC and the crashing of a jet in Pennsylvania. Since that day, for the past five years, our country and many others have reacted in various ways to those events.

This reminds me of the story of one of the Buddha's disciples, Ahimsaka, the non-violent one, a monk of profound insight and understanding. The story of Ahimsaka is recounted in a short book titled <u>The Buddha and the Terrorist</u> by Satish Kumar. In one lifetime a vicious killer called Angulimala became transformed into Ahimsaka, a morphing of determined murderer into a devout protector of life.

Angulimala was the name given to this murderer because after he killed men he would take their fingers and string them on a necklace, mala, and wear the bloodied fingers, anguli, around his neck. As the story goes Angulimala is eventually converted to Buddhism and follows the Buddha, transforming his life and becoming famous for non-violence and profound insight and understanding.

The book, however, is about more than this transformation, it is about what society does in reaction to the past deeds of the terrorist Angulimala and the devout disciple of the

Buddha Ahimsaka. In the story the King comes in search of Angulimala, not knowing that he had become a disciple of the Buddha. The King inters into a dialogue with the Buddha during which the Buddha tells the King,

> *"Your majesty, violence breeds violence. Revenge and justice are not the same. Someone, somewhere, needs to take the courage to break the cycle of violence. Forgiveness is superior to justice."*[1]

Today as we think about those events 5 years ago and what has happened until now we can find clear evidence of the truth that violence breeds only violence. In the past five years more Americans have been killed as a result of our efforts to punish terrorists than were killed on September 11, 2001. Even more innocent people in other countries have been killed. And still there is no end to terrorism. The violence has only led to more violence.

You might say well that is all well and good about non-violence, especially in the story since Angulimala renounced his violence. You may say that it is different in this case since the terrorists we are dealing with have not renounced their violence. Yet when the Buddha first approached Angulimala he did not do so on the precondition that Angulimala renounce violence. It was as a result of the Buddha's compassion towards the person Angulimala that this murderer was transformed into Ahimsaka the non-violent one.

So what do we do? As we think about the situation we may be tempted to think that it is bigger than us. We might

1   Satish Kumar, <u>The Buddha and the Terrorist</u>, (Green Books, 2004), p. 30

think that we have no say and are powerless to affect the changes worldwide by our solitary actions locally. When we think that way we fail to consider that terrorism, all terrorism, begins locally. We also fail to realize that ending suffering is the surest way to end terrorism, in whatever form it exists. However, it takes courage just as the Buddha told the king. Courage is needed because it is easy to become discouraged. If we become discouraged opportunities will pass us by.

In a book titled <u>Harp of Burma</u> by Michio Takeyama, The main character, in a letter to his former Captain during WWII writes,

> *"We Japanese have not cared to make strenuous spiritual efforts. We have not even recognized their value. What we stressed was merely a man's abilities, the things he could do [...]. Of perfection as a human being, of humility, stoicism, holiness, the capacity ... to help other... all of these virtues we were left ignorant."* [2]

The same thing can be said of us today as we listen to the news or read stories of the need to be "vigilant" or "resolved in our commitment" to fight terrorism. There is no teaching of compassion for those who are suffering.

In Pema Chodron's book <u>When Things Fall Apart</u> she recounts a cartoon she once saw. In the cartoon, "two women are standing behind their locked door peeking out the window at a monster standing on their doorstep. One of the ladies is saying, 'Calm down Edna. Yes, it is a giant

---

2 Michio Takeyama, <u>Harp of Burma</u>, (Tuttle Publishing 1996), p. 127

hideous insect, but it may be a giant hideous insect in need of help.'"[3] This is an example of the kind of courage it takes to face suffering and be willing to help alleviate it. It was the same courage and the same thinking that the Buddha had when he came into contact with the murderer Angulimala.

Tuesday, the day after 9/11 is the anniversary of the Tatsunokuchi persecution. This was when Nichiren was lead to the beach to be executed by beheading. With courage he faced this most significant trial for his belief in the Lotus Sutra.

Later as he was in exile on Sado Island he wrote several of his most important theoretical treatises.

In a few more days we will be entering the Higan season. This is a time for Buddhists to reflect on the six paramitas. I hope that each of us will take this opportunity to see the appropriateness of the Buddhas teaching for our time. I hope that we all look at the six paramitas and see how we can apply their guidance to solving the problems that exist in our lives and in society so that we can establish a peaceful society where all those who suffer will find comfort and compassion.

---

3 Pema Chodron, <u>When Things Fall Apart</u>, (Shambala, 2000), p. 25

Birth And Death – February 17, 2013 Meditation

Good morning. I hope everyone is doing well. Yesterday here in Charlotte we had some light snow showers. While it wasn't much I certainly enjoyed watching the snowfall. I appreciate what we had, though I wish it were more.

Friday was the 15th of February the day we commemorate the pari-nirvana of the Buddha. We don't know the exact day the Buddha died and so in various denominations and parts of the world different days are set aside to commemorate this event.

Saturday was the 16th of February, the day we commemorate the birth of Nichiren, born as Zennichi-maro in Kominata Japan. We know from historical records that he was the son of a fisherman.

So in one weekend we commemorate two events that highlight the cycle of life beginning with birth and ending with death. In between we experience life itself.

It is interesting to note that we normally engage in a lot of planning for birth and almost none for death. The stuff in between, life, may or may not be attended to.

"They will be reborn before the Buddhas of the

worlds of the ten quarters. They will always hear
this sutra at the places of their rebirth. Even when
they are reborn among men or gods, they will be
given wonderful pleasures. When they are reborn
before the Buddhas, they will appear in lotus
flowers." (Lotus Sutra, Chapter, page 203)

When there is a birth a lot of effort is sometimes put into the arrival of the new life. Sometimes rooms are painted in various colors, which are deemed appropriate to the baby. Clothes are purchased, special beds, and all sorts of equipment are obtained such as strollers, bottles, diapers, and so forth.

The arrival of a new life is greeted with great fanfare and celebration in most cases, though certainly not always.

Then there is life, the stuff in between. In life we go to school, learn many things and prepare for a life of productivity and reward. We study diligently, or perhaps not so much, and ready ourselves for a period of work in order to support our family or provide the necessities of life.

"There are always the sufferings of birth, old age,
disease and death. They are like flames raging
endlessly." (Lotus Sutra, Chapter III, page 77)

Some may also engage in a spiritual practice in order to cultivate peace and meaning for our lives. For those of us who practice Buddhism we meditate, or in the case of Nichiren Buddhists we chant the Odaimoku. Our ultimate objective is to attain enlightenment in this lifetime.

Taking care of our health is challenging for many. Eating right and getting exercise are some of the things we may try to engage in to hopefully minimize the effects of aging.

Then comes death, the thing we prepare for the least. We live our lives as if it were endless, and turn our backs on death. Out of fear perhaps, we do not wish to look death directly in the eye.

I have on several occasions lately spoken about or written about preparing for death. Some of these preparations include thinking about how we may wish to die, what kinds of care we wish to have provided. Making decisions about what life prolonging measures we wish to have done to us is prudent at any age.

> *''I am your great leader. I know that the bad road, which is made of birth-and-death and illusions, is dangerous and long, and that we should pass through it and get off it.'' (Lotus Sutra, Chapter VII, page 149)*

While we may not know the time of death or the way we will die, it is as important to make preparations for that time just as we prepare for the beginning of life. We may require the assistance of others in death just as we required support in birth. Considering who will support us and what we expect of them is crucial.

I hope that you will think seriously about death. Putting as much thought into death as we do into living is crucial. To die with the Odaimoku as our last breath can best be achieved if we have made preparations for this natural phase of life.

A Wisdom Talke

A Wisdom Tale – August 12, 2012 Meditation
United Nations International Youth Day

In 1999 the United Nations adopted resolution setting
aside August 12 as International Youth Day, and the first
celebration was held on August 12, 2000. This day is
designated as a day for governments and others to draw
attention to youth issues worldwide.

Today I am going to share with you a wisdom story, which
though, not directly speaking of Buddhism does have
application to those who practice the Lotus Sutra in this
age.

A very long time ago a recluse had a vision at his desert
monastery. In this vision he saw before him a vast ocean.
On one of the shores there was a monk standing at ocean's
edge. Suddenly the monk jumps high into the air and
spreads wings to catch the air. His brightly colored wings
caught the air and the monk soared effortlessly across this
large body of water. Soon he landed on the other shore and
walked inland to a heavenly land.

While the hermit was considering the meaning of this
strange revelation another monk appears on the shore
where the previous monk had started from. This monk also
leaps into the air, spreads his wings and begins to make

his way across the vast ocean. The monk this time did not have such an effortless journey, it required great physical exertion, but eventually the monk landed safely and entered the heavenly land.

Finally a third monk appears on the shore where the previous two had begun their journey. This third monk also launches himself into the air, spreads wings and begins the trip over the ocean. This monk however had a very hard time, he was smaller than the previous two, his wings required great effort to maneuver. Frequently he would nearly crash in the now choppy waters of the ocean; surely he would have drowned. Each time though he managed to beat his wings harder and rise up again. He struggled, and the hermit could tell it was taking its toll on the flying monk. Finally though the monk did reach the shore, he was so exhausted he could hardly stand, he looked half dead.

When the visions ceased the hermit went to his teacher to inquire into a possible meaning of these visions.

The teacher told him the first monk represents those believers who aspire to heaven in the present time, when religion and good people are everywhere, and reaching heaven is easy.

The second monk represents those who wish to reach heaven in the future years, for those in that time the journey will be difficult.

The third monk represents those in the distant future. It will be a time of great strife, religion will be rare and rarer still will be those who can correctly follow a spiritual path. During this time it will be very difficult to find one's way to the other shore.

The teacher then said, be glad you live in this time, but remember the third monk's efforts are worth much, much more than the efforts of all the rest.

This is exactly the message the Buddha taught in the Lotus Sutra. Those believers who were contemporaries of the historical Buddha had an easy time following the Buddha. There were fewer impurities among the people, and religion was easy to access. However in ages to come the practice becomes increasingly difficult. Finally in the age of the degeneration of the Dharma, in the ages very remote from the life of the Buddha it will be extremely difficult to practice. During that time there will be many misleading teachings, and the people will be impure and reject the Dharma.

As the Buddha says, in this age, the age in which we live, the age of the fifth five hundred years after the death of the Buddha, this is the time for the practice of the Lotus Sutra. Those who practice in this age will receive immeasurable merits far exceeding those of any previous practitioners.

Actively Engaged In Life

Actively Engaged In Life – August 23, 2012 Meditation

In a few days things will be changing gears as I begin a yearlong Chaplain residency program in a hospital here in Charlotte, NC. Back in December of last year I started writing daily meditation postings on my blog. My goal was to try to write and post every day something highlighting the Lotus Sutra.

Over these past eight months it was my intent to try to communicate to you the richness and depth of the Lotus Sutra as I have come to experience it. I do believe that we can find much to live by, much to be inspired by in this wonderful teaching of the Buddha.

The residency program is a full time undertaking working in the hospital every day and doing readings, writings and research in off times. My body and mind will be challenged in many ways.

Over the past couple of days I have been thinking about how to continue with my blog postings. I have wondered how they will be influenced by what I am engaging in and to what extent I might be able to share some of my experiences in a way that might be helpful. I haven't come up with a complete answer yet. Though some of it is falling into place.

One thing that I have been affected by so far in my Chaplain training revolves around Hope Theory and what that means and how it impacts every human. It became clear to me early on that without the Buddha understanding modern psychology the message of his teachings and the message of the Lotus Sutra tie in or satisfies some of the modern understandings of hope theory.

This is something that I would like to explore in more detail though I can't say at this point which directions it will take me. I would like to share this journey with you all. As I sit here writing and as I have processed this over the past week or so, I am guessing that I will share both theoretical explorations as well as encouragements much like I have this past year.

> *"To those who are confronted with sufferings, and tired of old age, disease, and death, the Buddha expounds the teaching of Nirvana, and causes them to eliminate these sufferings." (Lotus Sutra, Chapter I)*

Realizing that we are suffering causes us to awaken to the desire to end suffering. If we think that we will never experience suffering any more because we practice Buddhism would be a further delusion. Our journey of walking the path of Buddhist practice is not so much to avoid suffering but to participate in life so fully that we are truly awake to the impact of suffering and its causes in our lives.

If we seek to run from suffering as an end to suffering, if we do not open our life to the reality of suffering thinking that if only we practice Buddhism we will be immune to this truth of life then this only leads to false expectations and more suffering.

The truth of suffering is the immersion in life both joy and suffering. Being awake to 'this is suffering' and 'this is not suffering' requires us to participate, to experience but not to grasp, not to cling to one or the other. We are not innocent third part observers detached from our lives in the hope to avoid suffering.

> *"I will cause all living beings to cross the ocean of birth and death if they have not yet done so. I will cause them to emancipate themselves from suffering if they have not yet done so. I will cause them to have peace of mind if they have not yet done so."*
> *(Lotus Sutra, Chapter V)*

Community, It's Not About You

Community, It's Not About You – June 17, 2012 Meditation

In Buddhism, as I am sure you all know quite well, we have the Three Jewels. These three Jewels are the treasure in Buddhism and in our Buddhist lives. Buddha, Dharma, Sangha are these three jewels, without which there could be no Buddhism and without which our Buddhist practice becomes at best difficult.

It stands to reason why the Buddha is treasured, without our teacher there would be no Buddhism. The Buddha did not practice to attain enlightenment for himself, ultimately he turned his discovery outward. We can say, in a way, that the Buddha in that first teaching manifest the concept of Sangha, even from his first awareness that enlightenment was not something solely for himself.

The Sangha, as manifest by the entire universe, was witness to and present at the very moment of his enlightenment. So in a sense the Sangha, the enlightenment of the Buddha, and further the truth of Buddhism all occurred simultaneously.

Sometimes we may wish to separate these three, even going so far as to say the Sangha wasn't evident until the Buddha approached his fellow ascetics and gave his first teaching to which they became the Buddha's disciples. And of course that is perhaps the first physical manifestation of the appearance of Sangha. But in reality the Sangha was always there.

Sometimes people say to me, I wish I had a Sangha to practice with, or there is no one around me to join in my practice, or even I am all alone. There is of course some measure of truth to these claims, in that no one appears to be sitting beside you when you chant Odaimoku or recite the Sutras. But this is only on aspect of Sangha, perhaps the 'self' aspect because it in the thinking process it begins with and resides principally revolving around self or individual.

But Sanghas are not single individuals, they are community, they are other. I have heard people say, well I don't like so and so in my Sangha, or I would rather practice at home because I like my internet connections better, or they make me feel good. Again these are all self-centric. The beginning thought and the ending thought is about oneself, and further how others can be used to benefit one's self.

> *"The merits of the fiftieth person who rejoices at hearing this Sutra of the Lotus Flower of the Wonderful Dharma are immeasurable, limitless, asamkhya. Needless to say, so are the merits of the first person who rejoices at hearing this sutra in the congregation." (Lotus Sutra, Chapter XVIII)*

There is of course the aspect of Sangha that serves to support the individual, but that is only part of the equation. Perhaps the greatest part is what you as an individual contribute to the Sangha. Instead of the focus being on what you can take away from the Sangha and whether or not it meets your criteria, or serves to directly benefit you, the focus should equally if not more so perhaps be on what you can contribute to, what you can give to, what you can bring to the Sangha in the form of your presence.

> *"Thereupon the gods rained mandarava-flowers,*
> *maha- mandaravaflowers, manjusaka-flowers,*
> *and maha-manjusaka-flowers upon the Buddha*
> *and the great multitude. The world of the Buddha*
> *quaked in the six ways. The great multitude*
> *of the congregation, which included bhiksus,*
> *bhiksunis, upasakas, upasikas, gods, dragons,*
> *yaksas, gandharvas, asuras, garudas, kimnaras,*
> *mahoragas, men, nonhuman beings, the kings of*
> *small countries, and the wheelturning- holy-kings,*
> *were astonished." (Lotus Sutra, Chapter I)*

Another aspect of Sangha is the idea that everyone around you with whom you interact with is also your Sangha. You can provide care, support, encouragement, and example to many people in your life. In a sense stealth-teaching Buddhism. Your Sangha is not just who shows up at your door, but who you relate to in your life and how you value those connections and how you nurture those interactions.

> *"The hundreds of thousands of billions of living*
> *beings in this congregation like me followed the*
> *past Buddhas and received their teachings in their*
> *consecutive previous existences. They will respect*
> *and believe you. They will he able to have peace*
> *after the long night and obtain many benefits."*
> *(Lotus Sutra, Chapter II)*

Mission – Monday July 16, 2012 Meditation
Rissho Ankoku Ron submitted to Regent of Japan – 1260

"The more I've thought about happiness, the more
surprised I've been at the importance of the "atmosphere
of growth." I think this is a huge engine of happiness, and
when you have a mission, you create an atmosphere of
growth whenever you pursue that mission.

Have you found a way to have a mission? What is it –
and does it boost your happiness?" (Gretchen Rubin, The
Happiness Project <link http://happiness-project.com/
happiness_project/2012/07/want-to-have-more-fun-go-on-
a-mission/>)

When Nichiren submitted the Rissho Ankoku Ron to the
Japanese Regent in 1260 it was not for the purpose of
establishing a state sponsored religion. His intent was not
to force his beliefs on anyone. His intent was to present his
interpretation of the teachings of the Buddha and propose
a solution to the sufferings being experienced by the
Japanese population.

In the three year period prior to Nichiren's submission
of the Rissho Ankoku Ron over half of the population of
Japan had died either due to famine, natural disasters, or

disease. His motivation was to look for and offer a solution to end the sufferings of not just the people of Japan directly but all the people throughout the world indirectly.

His belief was that because the people had abandoned the correct teaching and had taken up with incorrect teachings the entire country had fallen victim to the three poisons of Buddhism; greed, ignorance, and anger. It wasn't just that the people were following incorrect teachings but that the government was sponsoring those who were misleading the people. His solution was two-fold. Ideally of course he hoped that the people when provided factual information about the teachings of the Buddha would change their practices. Second he urged the government to stop sponsoring religions.

Nichiren from the point of his submission of the Rissho Ankoku Ron endured many persecutions because of his beliefs. He also engaged in numerous debates with religious leaders of his time. He was such a skilled debater that one of the icons used to represent him is a debating stick used during formal debates. Time after time when allowed to present the facts of the teachings of the Buddha Nichiren proved his opponents wrong.

It seems that the more he proved the correctness of his position the more people it angered and the more he was persecuted.

> *"I am the King of the Dharma. I expound the Dharma without hindrance. I appeared in this world in order to give peace to all living beings."*
> *(Lotus Sutra, Chapter III)*

I began today with a recent web article on mission. I thought it was interesting especially since today we are talking about what Nichiren viewed his mission to be and what the mission of the Buddha was.

In both cases it was not for personal fame or profit, it was solely to enable all living beings to become happy, if they so chose. The Buddha never forced nor coerced anyone to follow his teachings. Nichiren likewise never did either. In fact when Nichiren was offered state support, the construction of state sponsored temples and government endorsement he walked away from the offer.

Today as we reflect on these two influential figures I wonder how we view the purpose or mission of our own lives. Do we see our function as one of mere existence or something of greater purpose?

It isn't necessary to be a great person to do great things, frequently it is ordinary people with a clear purpose in their lives to help others who do the most, even if they do not get top billing in the news.

From the quote above: "Have you found a way to have a mission?"

Connect with Ryusho Jeffus on-line:

Twitter:
@ryusho @myoshoji

Facebook:
https://www.facebook.com/Ryusho

Facebook Author Page:
https://www.facebook.com/revryusho

Blog:
https://www:ryusho.org/blog

Amazon Author Page
https://tinyurl.com/y6z9rcbm

Made in the USA
Middletown, DE
30 January 2025

70565051R00046